Revelations
Africa in Poetry

Munyaradzi Mawere

Langaa Research & Publishing CIG
Mankon, Bamenda

Publisher
Langaa RPCIG
Langaa Research & Publishing Common Initiative Group
P.O. Box 902 Mankon
Bamenda
North West Region
Cameroon
Langaagrp@gmail.com
www.langaa-rpcig.net

Distributed in and outside N. America by African Books Collective
orders@africanbookscollective.com
www.africanbookcollective.com

ISBN: 9956-791-61-X

DISCLAIMER
All views expressed in this publication are those of the author and do
not necessarily reflect the views of Langaa RPCIG.

Dedication

To my beloved brother, Cephas
Thanks for the inspiration!

Table of Contents

Preface.. vii

Poetry Revelations.................................... 1
A true mother 3
True love... 5
That flies lands....................................... 7
Shall we say the war is over?...................... 8
Labor pains.. 10
Who shall come to our rescue? 12
The end time.. 13
A prayer for forgiveness............................ 14
Home coming... 16
The winding path.................................... 18
Diasporians... 20
A snake in the house................................ 22
The chameleon's wish............................... 24
Pedro.. 26
T3.. 27
A treacherous twin brother
Zimpeto.. 30
The jiri.. 32
A continent called Africa........................... 34
Fear no more.. 35
While the sun shine.................................. 37
The story of my life.................................. 38
Yes... 43
Dear sister... 45
Death of the tyrant.................................. 46
Time... 48

If I am to live.. 49

Exiled mind.. 50

Unpredictable world.. 51

At the well.. 52

Permanence of change.................................... 54

Across the Limpopo River............................... 55

School drop-outs... 56

The cyclone... 57

To my son James.. 58

Hero... 60

God bless Africa.. 62

All started with marriage.................................. 64

Afghanistan Vista.. 65

A cry for freedom.. 67

On the death bed... 68

Children of Africa.. 70

The way it is.. 72

Treacherous species.. 73

Street Kid... 74

Troubles of my heart....................................... 76

At the mine... 79

By the Indian Ocean.. 80

Babies of this world... 82

November 2008... 83

June 2008... 85

What they say I am.. 87

Before sunrise... 89

When love dies.. 91

To my husband, Farai....................................... 93

The reply to my wife, Chipo............................. 98

Corruption.. 102

New media technology..................................... 104

My life as a woman... 106
Death of the rural home............................... 107
Worlds of this world..................................... 109
Harurwa.. 110
African City... 111
Up there.. 113
Untied tongues.. 115
All that flies fly to land? 116
Language injustice....................................... 119
Death... 121
A prophecy of revolution............................ 123
Children of chaos.. 125
Fools.. 127
Songs from the forests................................ 129
Africa voice... 131
2013 Catastrophe.. 133
Where are you policemen?........................... 135

Preface

This book is a diverse, impeccable collection of poems that strive to render insights on and acknowledge the theoretical and practical potentialities of poetry in questioning and reflecting on the realities of life. The book expresses with great legerdemain a gamut of issues, desirable and undesirable alike such as dissipation, corruption, war, love, bad governance, greediness, anxiety, religion, weather, time, politics, morality, economics, justice, natural environment and culture: socio-economic and political issues that trouble, boggle and dishearten humanity across the world.

With its incisive but rigorous studious excursion on the theoretical and practical potentialities of poetry to penetrate all spheres of life and reveal the truths beneath, this book powerfully and aptly questions a wide spectrum of situations. The volume is an expression of the author's passion for a 'good life' to all- a life in which all pragmatic strategies aimed at addressing the problematic concerns of humanity are reflected upon and brought to light. As such, this book is a penetrating and refreshing expose` steeped in candour and sincerity as it brings together poems of different dimensions in an intellectual fait accompli worthy of inclusion in one cherished collection.

For lovers of poetry, cognoscenti, students and instructors of English Literature, this is a must-read text!

Poetry Revelations

Poetry!
A powerful weapon of the oppressed and the troubled
Was it born out of a woman
The same way children are born?

Real poetry!
Through decades of slave trade
And centuries of colonialism
With the sons of the soil bound in chains
All in chains
Feeding on the bitterness of their tears
And the sourness of their sweat
Poetry was born

In the walls of Amsterdam
And walls of the oppressed land
Full of metaphors of agony
Full of symbols of hatred
And racism and apartheid
Poetry was born

Real poetry!
It is bold, a revelatory expression
Of the agonized tormented minds
Beleaguered by the oppressor's heartless feelings
And noxious deleterious zeal to perpetrate injustice
Against the innocent souls
Souls of fellow others

Poetry was born

Real poetry!
It is resisting flavor
Courage that the haunted souls garner
To resist the injustices imposed on them
And the freedom denied of them

Real poetry!
For as long as the oppressor lives
Injustice pitted against the innocent
Wars waged against defenseless civilians
Intellects of the fair minded persevere
It shall live long life
To interpret the grievances, tribulations and feelings of the oppressed
And the concerns of the troubled
To put on the open poetry revelations
Revelations that emerge from the profound depths of silence
And immeasurable aptitudes of the talented minds

A true mother

(For Maria, my aunt)

To whom I owe more than I can say by word of mouth
The unwavering delight, stanch and resolute
The untiring love, determined and unconditional
The rhythm of warm comfort, reposed and soothing
A true mother among mothers!

Of your sweat I fed
Of your comfort I relaxed
Of your love I enjoyed
A true mother among mothers!

Your love no peevish whirlwind shall blow
No sullen desert sun shall wither
Your comfort no mugger shall steal away
Not even the singe desert weather shall shrivel
Nor sultry sun of the equator shall take away
A true mother among mothers

Your character determined and unshakeable
Itself alone teach more than a teacher
Itself alone enough to teach a fool
A true mother among mothers!

This is a dedication to you mother
For you, now and forever
Private words addressed to you in public
For others to learn of your good ways

For others to learn of your good character
For others to learn of your loving heart
A true mother among mothers!

True love

Though I value the dignity of human life
To the extent that I preach its sacredness in the open
That I serve it in the hospitals
That I nurture it in the schools
If all this is done on condition
I am a hypocrite
It is not true love

Though I can move from one community to the other
Selling my manifesto that approve of the goals of human
liberation
A manifesto that profess love for human freedom
If this is done on condition
I am a hypocrite
It is not true love

Though I can buy my family all the necessities
To move on with life
Sending all my children to school
And smile as I give them offerings
If this is done on condition
I am a hypocrite
It is not true love

Though I can teach love in the churches and schools
Preaching love in loud voice
If this is done on condition
I am a hypocrite

This is not true love

True love is unconditional
It rejoices in the struggle for the good
It preserves amidst all evil
Surrendering not to the will of the devil

True love never fades away
For it hopes and persists
Amidst all gross injustices
It sprouts even in winter
When malicious weather strikes

True love perseveres to conquer
To replace injustice with justice
Hurt with love
Wrong with right
Enmity with affability

True love respects
For true love loves freely

True love is faithful
For true love lives without doubt
And leaves an enduring legacy of goodness

To all those to come!

That flies lands

Little do we know
To whom these words are directed

Ferocious darkness fills all land
Night falls all day to give no chance to day
Violent night forgetting that it comes to go
To relieve the wracked souls of their agony
And the tired bodies of their weariness

Silent voices restless and mourning
Filling all the sky and heavens beyond
Hiding from us
The nostalgia and melancholy of those gone

We long to sing joy
In the sunrise
Yet like morning dew that evaporates on sunrise
And winter clouds that disappear on midday

And meat smoke that scatters so instantaneously
Everything goes the same way
For nothing comes to stay
Nor flies high not to land again

Shall we say the war is over?

Yesterday
We bore and raised soldiers and not children
Soldiers to defend the sovereignty of our country
And the dignity of our heritage
All in the name of sovereignty

The liberation struggle
Off it went
To bring freedom
Freedom to bear and raise children
Not soldiers
Freedom to bear and raise heirs
Not deserters
But what freedom
For the war is not over?

Again,
We are only free to bear and raise school goers
Soldiers of another kind
Not children
To bear and raise apostates
Not heirs
To bear and raise hooligans
Not the incorruptibles

We toil for their education
To nurture their intellects
With all good hope
That they hand over the memo to the next generation

Watching them growing

Both mentally and physically
But for how long a time?
Only epigrammatic a moment
For soon they leave
Off to the city
Off to the west
All they go!

Waving backwards as if they come back tomorrow
Only to leave us in downright despair
As our sons and daughters during the liberation struggle
Off they went
Promising and promising
To come back before long
As if they knew war would end soon

Some went
Never to come back
Others went
Only to come back bones
More others went
Only to come back grey

Again,
Their sons and daughters go
Preaching the same gospel: 'Soon we will be back'
Shall we then say the war is over?

Labor pains

A declaration from the Creator:
'To the woman, I will greatly multiply your pain in childbearing
In pain you shall bring forth children'
All this as punishment for deceit

1 O'clock in the afternoon
I was there by the walls of the labor house
Waiting to hear the news from inside
There I sat leaning the walls of the labor house

It required no instructor to call for attention
For what came through the walls of the labor house
Was itself enough to call my attention

I could feel the whimpering callings for the midwives
Penetrating through the thick walls of the labor house
Some yelling: 'Mbuya! may I go to the toilet?'
Others shrieking: 'Mbuya! come nearer it now wants to come out!'

From the other side of the walls
I could hear the voices of the midwives, charged
Penetrating through the thick walls of the labor house
'Hey you stay there! You will go to the toilet only under my instruction!'
'Hey be steady! Who told you it now wants to come out?'
It appears there was pandemonium, mayhem in the house

As all mothers, expecting were yelling, groaning in agony

Then I began to wonder lost in imagination, seated:
'But if labor pains are all this painful
Why these women run after men even for the second, third,
forth, and....
To receive these substances that will ultimately send them to
the seventh heaven of pain?'

Many answers came, presenting themselves before me one by
one
One voice came: 'It's really painful dear, the most painful
experience any person can ever have
Only that women are so committed to fulfill the command of
God
That in pain a woman shall bring forth children'
Hear the other voice: 'Ah, it's not all that painful as the
sounds from the labor house purport
For if it was so no woman would go after a man after her first
birth
It's not painful a duty but only that women are hen-hearted
creatures, fearful'

As other voices trickle in, distraction!
I was ordered by the senior nurse to vacate the walls
And off I went, away from the walls of the labor house
Lost in profundities of imagination

Who shall come to our rescue?

We stagger in the darkness
Our steps falter
Anesthetizing in fear
Our voices cry in agony, deafening
Only unfilled nighty voices
Pulsate in the reverberation of demise

We stagger in the mist zone in search for places of hope in today's context
As the mist fills the whole land
Our voices cry in agony, deafening again
Craving for the itch to get all the luxury
But alas!
Our humanity is gone
Our dignity is perished
Leaving behind the chaff, we cry!

Only unfilled nighty voices
Pulsate in the reverberation of demise

We stagger in circle in the pelt rain
As the rain storms heavy from the northwest
Our voices cry in agony, earsplitting
Only unfilled nighty voices
Pulsate in the reverberation of demise

We should all agree
That our future is bleak
In as much as we are not rescued

The end time

The time is approaching
The time of truth
Real truth charged like maddened bull
But all urging to win
Never to hear the loss of end

The time is approaching
The time with meaning so varying
The time with many interpreters
Lacking the courage sufficient to face the end
Many a people stumble on a guess
Uncertain of what the future is in store of them

We have all come, that's certain to us all
We will all go, that's certain to us all
Time is running to its end, that's certain to us all
To take us out of sight, that's certain to us all
To where exactly is the grand question
For that is not certain to us all
And will remain hidden
Till "D- Day" comes!

A prayer for forgiveness

Forward looking!
I think of nothing but a strong wire of eternity
That leads to a place peaceful and all roses
A place of glory and purity

That place far!
That only hails the pure in heart
That only calls over the ambassadors of love
The torch bearers to the blind
Preservers of eternity

I pray therefore I pray
That if I wronged you, you forgive my spirit
That if I betrayed you, you summon your love
That you forget my errors of the past
That set us apart, asunder
For to you and me
Eternity is not possible without love
The nourishment to the heart and all life

To forgive is more worthwhile
Than to nurse a grudge
To smile to a betrayer is more worthwhile
Than to mourn for a broken promise

Much in life stands in our way
Nourished and nurtured by a loving heart that forgives
For a heart that forgives is like sun

That lights us our way when we wrong and go astray
To salver the lost faltering in darkness

Home coming

The motherland is singing
Far, far away far
Calling the scattered sheep
From far north, far south, far east, far west
The motherland is calling, wailing
For the scattered sheep are too many a children
Too many to come and pose for a kiss
And suck the deserted tits of dried breasts
Or break into a stage dance on arrival

I see all as they come
Some hesitant, their destinies still a million uncertainties
Their eyes still filled with tears
Silent, desperate and wet tears

I see all as they come
Some drunk with the sting of loss
The loss they incurred in their motherland
And the wild screams they screeched that night
Crying crazily like cockroaches crawling on canes

I see all as they come
Some tired and weary of broken promises
Promises that nurtured their wounds
And shattered their invisible river hope between them

I see all as they come
Some thinking of the love they left behind in motherland

The love of their mothers and lovers
That warmed their bodies and the feelings beneath
All leaping flames of longing ravage
Home coming!

The winding path

Life!
A winding path
With many phases

To get there you pass through many gates
That all have gate keepers to devour or spare you

From the womb
It is born
To grow in this limited space
A space so paradoxical!
Some say:
It's a mixed bag
Others say:
Everything goes
Happiness
Sorrow
Success
Failure
All in one world!

That's life
But leading where in this limited space-vanity?
Nobody seems to know
Some say:
To the oceans-to the world underneath
Others say:
Down to the deep soils-to line up with the ancestors

Yet others say:
Up up - to the sky and heavens beyond to reunite with the
Creator
Whichever way
The journey though not equally long
Is long
It is indeed a winding path!

Diasporians

'Diasporians' – back home they call you
For them you are sparkling gold
Achievers of finest shares
Masters of victory
But are you really what they say?

Contrary to your people
They call you with all derogatory names
Lampooning and caricaturing your persona
Go to the south- they call you '*makwerekwere*'
In the east- they call you '*zvingondo*'
Far abroad- you are fortune seekers
Man of no fixed aboard
Pursuers of good life and tantalizing hopes

Now you are grey headed
But still with undying hope
Unquenched thirst
And unsatiated hunger
Seeking tantalizing fortunes
That like rainbow colors you will never get hold of

Loses come and go
But you are unmoved for you are faithfully groomed
Fortunes come and go

But all to renew your determination
You are ever 'Diasporians'

And never permanent citizens

When will you become?
How will you become?
For you are a fortune seeker that is never turned a fortune
man
A man of no fixed aboard that will always be called?

The number of grey hair in your head multiply day by day
Wrinkles on your face shrinking as you swallow bread
morsels
And your body muscles loosen like barren soils of Sahara
To bare your age
Yet still a man of no fixed aboard you remain
With blood-felt desire to settle
Only when the disturbed waters settle
Or destiny decides your fate
Diasporians!

A snake in the house

Brother!
This is a snake in the house
A real venomous snake!

From a distance
It glittered
Shining with dazzling brilliance like gold particles in day light
Oh shi-i!
But was it real gold?

A pinch of it tasted sweet
Like honey of the forest, of the small bees
Those bees we call "*dendende*"
But ye-h,
Beware, sure beware!

Others encouraged you to pick it up
To take it home for life
This terrible snake, retrogressive, remorseless!
But was it their faulty for little did they know
That indeed it was a snake- a real venomous snake?

Though I have always been suspicious
Of its chameleonic behavior
So spasmodic and erratic like weather of the sea
Unforgiving!
And I warned
Brother this is a snake- a venomous snake!

But you did not listen
Neither did you consult your elders
And you never dared to study its colors!

Attractive but repelling
Encouraging but discouraging
All in the glitters
Glitters of a python to a prey
You were lured

Now where are the "glittering colors"
The tenderness falsely manifested?
For even a blind man can now afford;
To see its true simulated colors
And even a deaf can now afford
To hear its true voice
A voice that utters no peace
A voice that speaks no good
A voice that knows no praise but curse
A voice that knows no boundary
That's why I say:
This is a snake in the house!

My grand question to you now is:
"What shall you do with this snake in the house?"

The chameleon's wish

It is not my wish
That I move slowly
Hesitantly
Beating the ground's warmth
Like all ground is hot porridge

It is not my desire
That I take hours to traverse the road
Sometimes trodden up before achieving my goal
To cross over to the other side

All is by custom
Habits of my ancestors
Their custom was never to hasten hastily
Nor to move forward instantly

My elders,
This they taught:
That I keep watch before my next step
That I watch my country-side before my next step
That I watch the earth I tread upon before I set foot
That I capture prey with my magnetic tongue
That I change my clothes a hundred times a day
That I think before I act
That I hold tightly on to my heritage

And, that I cross the river when I get there

Who then are you to instruct:
That I throw away my humanness like a fool throwing bath
water with the baby
That I scorn my own values like an unthinking zombie
That I disregard my elders like a hoodwinker
That I uproot my own roots like a foolhardy
That I deny my forefathers like a confused cockroach?
To hell with your hocus-pocus and hoity-toities!
Don't you know that a chameleon is a chameleon?
So I am, I remain one
That's my wish

Pedro

A friend indeed
That my heart cannot afford
Not only to forget
But to thank in words

I remember those days
My life in despair
With little if at all any hope

Like an angel you came by my side
To raise my life from the cemetery of hopelessness
Deep from the profound depths of desolation

Yes,
I remember those days
When seated under that shade outside the saloon
With my soul dejected, a running away persona
Only held back by your fascinating stories
Catching and absorbing
Your words not only comforting but helpful
Sweet and sweeter than honey

And with your words of encouragement
You singlehandedly raised
A hopeless life
From the deep cemetery of hopelessness
Look now
Here I am!

T3

In a tiny reed hut
A hut where merciless mosquitoes gathered all day
A hut where rats of all sizes gathered for a meeting every night
A hut where cockroaches claimed ownership
All as if in exchange of the rentals they did not receive

In this hut
Lived a life
Great but unrecognized
Torn and weary
Tired!
Of tantalizing hopes that never materialized
Waiting and waiting
For the rainy season
Bankrupt in solace
For phone calls that never rang
And surprises that never be
Imagining
Promises that never fulfilled

When does it come?
Perhaps inside that life
A little voice says: 'Patience pays, keep waiting!'
But for how long is the million dollar question
That even the little voice affords not a precise answer

A treacherous twin brother

Sired by the same father
Born of the same womb
Suck the same nipple
Ate from the same plate
And shared the same blanket
They grew up with the same strength
With the same spirit
And the same feelings

Like termites in summer
They were united
Faithful like the shadow in a sunny day
They stood for each other
In harmony they lived
Daring not to provoke
Worse to swindle

They loved each other to the bones
Fighting for common goals:
Success
Unwavering unity
Love for each other
Togetherness

Only until this day
The darkest hour
With a sudden turn away
Of a brother from a brother

All because of a woman
With a flickering tongue
That extinguishes burning fire
And radiates lightning sparks

Where is the true love?
Can true love of brotherhood evaporate so easily like morning dew?
Can it disperse so quickly like winter clouds
Can it wilt in midday like a flower rose
Or fade skyward staggering like a smoke cloud?

Some say: it's charm
Others say: it's love for woman
Whatever they call it
It never ceases to be treachery
A treacherous twin brother!

Zimpeto

3 O'clock in the afternoon
It all started!

Booming guns
Whistles of lethal bombs
Filling the air with deafening noises
Making the countryside to roll and lull
And bellies of the adults to shamelessly parade their
gastronomic secretes
All out of fear

Echoes of piercing cries of agony all over
Contracting the muscles of all body
And twinges the veins of all head

Stunned and scared
The survivor of the explosions
He sat, knelt, prayed
For God to decide his fate

The evil of weapons of mass destruction!
Like the bombs of Nagasaki
They filled the air
Grenades whizzed over his dead-nerved body
Huddled like a bundle of sticks around a banana tree
His heart pounding
His blood playing hip-hop
His hair, all in akimbo

As if to fly away from where it all grew

Running!
Not a solution at all
For this was God's case
Besides,
The angry grenades and charged automatic riffles
All ran faster than all men

Looking!
Everywhere all bodies
Scattered and unmoved
Finished by the merciless weapons of mass destruction
As they toiled and labored to their last
He only survived
To tell the tale!

The jiri

A place so amazing
Where the sun rises not!
Nor sun rays penetrate forth!
The jiri

It cools in the jiri
For fresh air always blow
Rivers always flow
A place full of life

It is peaceful in the jiri
For neither fight nor quarrel prevail
Only gentle talks

It is safe in the jiri
For men and animals are friends
Fear not
No harm

It is resource bound in the jiri
For it is full of delicious harurwa

It is joyous in the jiri
For you hear only melodious voices of colorful birds
And gentle buzzing of busy bees

It is refreshing in the jiri
For you watch sweet smelling roses

And hear the chattering of monkeys
A Garden of Eden in the savanna lands
Where all biodiversity mingle
Peacefully greeting each other
Oh blessed you are
The jiri

A continent called Africa

The cradle of mankind
Rich in everything
Riches and poverty
The good and the bad
The best and the worst

Where does this paradox recline?
In slave trade
In colonialism
In globalization
In poor governance
In lack of strategic framework of your own
Where?

Fear no more

Clear your heart
Of all fear
Anxiety
And sorrow

Clear away all your tears
Soft and tender like morning dew
Dropping gentle to wet the dry land
Fear no more

Open your arms in embrace
In joy
For the sun will surely rise

Like flower buds in the season of spring
Your hope will regenerate
Dazzling
Like sun's brightness

Fear no more
For the whirlwind of change has come
To replace:
Tear with joy
Cry with laughter
War with peace
Injustice with justice
Bad with good
And to devour all fear around

Fear not
Therefore fear no more!

While the sun shine

While the sun shine
And your age still run tender
And your wits still run sharp
And your energy still moves the hills
And your conviction drill a diamond rock
And your tongue a pebble of small bee honey

While the sun shine
Dazzling with brilliance
And sparkling with shining rays
Make hay
For this is the time!

The story of my life

I

Morning comes
Day goes
Promising
As it sinks down beyond the Siyawatonga mountains

Next morning comes
Round sun rises with inviting warmth
All its dazzling beautiful colors shining
All birds singing to welcome the new day

At the heart of the day
The mountains are neither taller nor shorter than their shadows
Yet the sun burns pitifully
Breeze blows with serenity
Promising!

At dusk the peaceful warmth, breeze and light
Bring the night together on the western side of Siyawatonga mountains
All combining to form a wonderful unforgettable evening

Everything was well until that night, the black night
That brought to its knees the economy of the land
With effects that nobody ever liked
The bourgeois, the workers and peasants alike
All cried the same voice

For a monster, terrible had invaded their territory
With promising desire to wreak havoc in the land

Realizing the new comer, not so long after its landing
I trembled in fear, that of the impending sufferings

My head between thighs, aching
My voice growling in consternation
My stomach rambling in sounds of all kinds
My blood boiling, circulating faster than hydroelectric motor
I knew the real enemy had come
An enemy that will spare no one
Good or bad
Rich or poor
Knowledgeable or ignorant
Wise or foolish

An enemy that resembles death but itself not death
An enemy that leaves no stone unturned
In its presence I survived
Into the fateful day

II

As the new day came
Ill-prepared I was
For the flamboyant and admirable life I desired

Not by my design
But by someone's design

That I couldn't prepare myself for a life
A life carved by decade-long of suffering and perseverance
A life carved by decade-long of mourning and sadness
A life carved by decade-long of socio-economic tribulations
A life carved by decade-long of political violence and merciless killings
A life carved by decade-long of force that resisted the momentum of progress
A life carved by decade-long of force that resisted the wishes and hopes of my ego
A life carved by decade-long of forces quivering with ego of a snake

The logic of oppositions, it resembled
With darkness striving to overpower light
With hatred striving to conquer love
With pain working against joy
With night refusing to give chance to day
With failure working against success
A totally new life with everything working against my will

The footprints of suffering!
Printed and scattered all over southern Africa and beyond
The source of my life:
Its form in Zimbabwe
Its fighting in Mozambique
Its zenith in South Africa

Thirsting for success
Good life!

Sinking in the deep valleys of imagination
Wondering in the groves and mountains of Nemahacha
Eating away the heart of my body
As I sat besides the Indian ocean with time-cuffed mind
Sometimes absorbed by the tidalectics and birds of the sea

In Zimpeto!
Seated in desperation
Watching the sky tire the sun
And the hands of the clock ticking like heart beat

In the tiny curved hut of T3
My blood bubbling and boiling
As I witnessed the merciless mosquitoes feasting on my sour
blood

In Matola, I languished in individual inferno
Thinking as each day passes sinking into the night
And giving me no hope

In Xai-Xai, my heart!
It gave a final push
To break away the troubling of chains around
Struggling for good life

III
The sun is rising again
This time slowly

Its dazzling brilliance faint

Looking eastwards!
I can see the sun
Like a flower bud of a wilting plant, frail
Struggling to spread its tentacles to attract the bees and beetles of the forest

Looking in the sky!
Some rain clouds but not as black as the 'real' rain clouds
 Northwest!
Violent wind, strong
Could this be a sign for the rains to cool the dry land
Or a sign of rebirth
Or a sign to sweep away the struggles of yesterday?

I can see all singing with joy
Others ululating and whistling

Looking aside!
The sckeptics, the so-called big brains
All reluctant to join in the celebration
As for them nobody knows

Could this be the real sun rising to shine
Or sun of the clouds, appear to disappear again into the clouds?

Yes

Voice: There is a woman
Chorus: Yes
Who trains
Yes
A brother to fight a brother
Yes

There is a man
Yes
Who trains
Yes
A sister to hate a sister
Yes

Where is this woman
Yes
Who makes a ring
Yes
For a brother to fight a brother?
Yes

Where is this man
Yes
Who prepares a breeding ground
Yes
For a sister to become an enemy of a sister?
Yes

Everywhere
Yes
They have read
Yes
That the woman of your house
Yes
Have put the family asunder
Yes

Everywhere
Yes
They have heard
Yes
That the man of your house
Yes
Have denied a sister and a sister to share
Yes

Since the woman came
Yes
Since the man came
Aaaaaaaaaah!

Dear sister

Yes, I heard the news!
Weakening and dispiriting though
Yet, little can I do
To present my physical body before you all back home
For hundred thousands of kilometers away I find myself

But though physically absent
In spirit I am present
The eye of my spirit gazes from a distance
To witness all the activities and problems that haunt you all

For what has more value my physical body or my spirit?
If it is the spirit as I believe
Then worry not
For I am always with you all back home

But if it is my body that value more
Worry not
I am on my way home
I am coming

Death of the tyrant

I hear the news
Broadcasted from the white house
That finally he is dead!

Thorn-bitten and in scene of carnage
The tyrant
The fearful figure

He who declared terror to all who refuse to yield to his power

He died
The exterminator of fellow humans!

He who beleaguered the innocent souls
And shrunk the spirits and hopes of his people
He who dispersed his people like a wolf amidst the sheep
And reduced them all to destitute,
He died!

Sure, he died!
Bathed in sorrow like a rodent

Caged deep down the ground
To escape the inescapable death

He died, no doubt he died
To cleanse the land he messed
And the tears that run down like the Nile

Yes, he died
Though against his will and determination
To oppress the blameless
To perpetrate injustice
To make his people live in perpetual fear
To make the hopes of his people a shattered dream

Truly, he died
I saw him buried deep down than usual
Into immeasurable depths of oblivion
He died
A laughing stock

Time

When seasons change
Everything changes
So are seconds, hours, days, weeks, months and years
Or time to be precise

Time seems to determine everything
But is it in control of itself?
Does it have all the power in itself?
To command seasons to fall into each other
Like interlocking mountains into a spur
And humans to go aging
While it determines its own forward moving

Through time's forward moving everything seems to follow:
The principle of regression
The principle of force
The logic of reduction
The logic of reasoning

In time
Everything seemingly goes
Good and bad
Right and wrong
War is fought for peace to prevail
Rain falls to cease, wiping drying the air
People are born to die
As night falls for day to triumph
For in time everything goes

If I am to live

If I am to live!
I must not live like a forest hare with no fixed aboard
Or a beggar that depends on grace
Or a warlord that satiates on bloodshed
Or a slave master that quenches his thirst with slave sweat
If I am to live!

If I am to live!
I must not live like a rabid dog cursed all life long
Or a donkey that works but buried unceremoniously when dead
Or a hen that scratches the ground all life long
Or a fool that draws water in reed basket all day long
If I am to live!

If I am to live!
I must live:
Peacefully
Lovely
Wisely
And Godly
With all dignity
And power to live
If I am to live!

Exiled mind

I am tired of an interminable war
Of peace that never is
Of hope that never materialize
Exiled mind in the present body

I am tired,
Of a long parallel waiting
Of acute anxiety
Swelling with fragrant hope

My body imprisoned
Bound in chains all over
Only to keep my mind
Roaming
Exiled
In a foreign land!

Unpredictable world

Every day I regret
Cursing the day my mother conceived
The period my mother nurtured my pregnancy
And the very day my life was casted to this world
A world so perfidious, treacherous
A world so unpredictable

Today here I am, hungry
Tomorrow there I am, feasting
Today free
Tomorrow in chains
Today employed
Tomorrow a destitute
Today enjoying company
Tomorrow lonely and deserted
Today happy
Tomorrow in rags of grief
All in one world: A world so treacherous
A world so unpredictable

Even when I ask: 'where am I?'
The answer is uncertain
For the world I find myself is all mystery
With nothing fixed: peace, war, freedom, oppression
All come and pass in one world
This world, unpredictable!

At the well

It all started at the well
Where I met her
Youthfulness in her face
Tenderness in her voice
Gentleness in her walk-pace
Her features immaculate

Her teeth white milk
Her eyes cute and shining
Her cheeks supple and limber
Her smile summer lightning
Penetrating, glowing, and radiating
Her voice soft and peaceful
A gem of creation!

There I stood
Baffled, stunned and perplexed
Blank - empty in dead silence
What to say?
Where to start from?

Her commodious ebony-smooth smile
A bogus chuckle!
Her soft response to my proposal
A complete surprise- a surprise that never ceases

My song she carried
Far to her aunt, aunt Chipo

That I am loved
So loved
Loved to the bones
By a man who comes from the people

Permanence of change

Little do we know
The deeper meaning of these words
Only after careful scrutiny we realize
That only change comes to stay
For nothing else comes to stay:
Night comes to fall perhaps unwillingly into day
So is silence to voice
And winter to summer
And heat to cold
And war to peace
And chaos to order
And youth to old age
For on this earth
All is swept away by the tide of change
Except the permanence of change
That will come and go
Only to come again and go

Across the Limpopo River

With hyenas on their trail, they marched on
With heavy rains pounding hammering on their bodies, they marched on
With empty stomachs gnawing, they marched on
With thirst burning their throats, they marched on
With vultures awaiting their death, they marched on
With fierce thorns piercing their bare feet, they marched on
With lions roaring ahead, they marched on
With high hopes flying on the horizon, they marched on
With crocodiles calling their names, they marched on
Across the hungry waters, they all marched

In their numbers they go
To a place far,
Far away from home
All hoping for good life
Further down
Down south

Some are rewarded
Others are cursed
The injustices of crossing over
And sojourning!

School drop-outs

From school, they drop
To fall headlong, when others go

They grow physically, when others grow intellectually
To become farm laborers, when others become doctors
To become housemaids, when others become nurses
To marry prematurely, when others marry maturely

At work, they toil all day
Only to get peanuts, a mockery to their laboring

In politics, they vote
But not to be voted by those they vote into office

In leadership, they praise
But not to be praised by those they praise

In development projects, they listen
But not to be listened by those they listen to

Is all this not enough to say: They fall when others go?

The cyclone

Whistling and gushing winds
Pelting hailstorm
Shattering the earth and the sky
Merging them to one as the echoes of the cyclone penetrates

From the countryside to the far reaching horizons
Charged like maddened bull, with sparks of cosmic fires that
quakes
 Devouring all life standing their way
All in the name of cyclone

The mountains!
All roared and lulled in deafening echoes

Animals of the forest run amok
Up and down the hills
Birds of the air
Fly wild, high to the zenith
Only to meet up the fierce drops of the hailstorm

People!
Like chicken in the face of an eagle, they huddle
Away from the ruthlessness of the mad cyclone
Only to find themselves in the open
Greeted by the fury of the cyclone eline!

To my son James

My son and only son!
When are you coming home?
Since you went away on that black night
Running away with your dear life far to the west
Hiding away from the unforgiving so-called economic woes

Your grandfather joined his ancestors 10 years down the line
I informed you of his passage
You only lamented but never did you promise to come
sooner or later

Your very father followed
Your sister, Rudo called
And you lamented, she said
But never did you promise to come sooner or later
Are you never home sick?

Now it's me
Smelling death,
Lonely,
Hungry,
Powerless,
Deserted,
With my spirit ceasing not to call
'James! James! My son!'
But again you show no sign
Neither do you promise
To come sooner or later

You cease not to amaze me
Neither do you cease to make me ill

Is it the city
Or the tall buildings that tour in the moonlight
Or the western education from the college
Or the golden papers I hear
That has stolen away your heart?

Hear my voice James!
Come! Come! come son!
Come!

Hero

My mind is always boggled
Boggled by one big question
A question I am sure does not haunt me alone:
The question of heroism-what a hero is?
Or who should be considered a hero on this land?

On this land they say:
A hero is one who fought in the struggle for liberation against colonialism
For them none except liberation fighters deserve this golden name
But could this be true, fair, and just,
That heroism ended with national independence?
That heroism only deserves those who took up arms?

Would we all go by the false logic
That if colonialism didn't come
Then no one could have been a hero?

Rational and fair minds would say: 'No'
Heroes and heroines have always been there
Before and during the liberation struggle
And they shall always exist alongside time and circumstances

Not only politicians deserve the name, 'hero'
For a hero is a genius
Not only a genius in war and politics
But in any humane endeavor

That seeks to improve the lives of many

Hi-i, hi-i, hi-i, I lament!
For many heroes and heroines have fallen
Silently and unrecognized-the unsung heroes and heroines
Sons and daughters of the soil
Others are still falling
Having achieved many a great thing for the great masses

Things that politicians and warlords fail
Not because they lack the will
But because they lack the genius complexity for excellence
So who deserves,
The golden name: 'Hero or Heroine?'

God bless Africa

The sun rise
The cock crows
Skin color that symbolized enmity crumples into powdery
dust
All smeared in one color
All are brothers and sisters: the so-called black, white, red,
yellow and colored
All beyond the boundary of color

Rejoice in the new day
Bathe yourself in the morning dew
Feel the warmth of the sunshine
And enjoy the gentle breeze from the mountains

Go down there to the river
Bathe the smell of your body
That for years was smeared with blood

Let your joy replace the bitterness of your tears
Let your songs cleanse the bruises of your body
That survived the tribulations and inflictions of the bullet
flames
And pain, that for years was stored in the depths of your
hearts

Let warmth of this day and earth mingle with the sound of
the flowing waters

Let rain cleanse dust of the gunshots that muzzled the air
Let breeze from the mountains blow
To cool the air that for years was sprinkled by the sparks of
grenades

Drive your thought back to the old days, but not for any bad
And remember:
How life was declared valueless by the brutal gunshots
How you were denied the right to till the land of your
forefathers
How you were taught to hate your own brother
How you were taught to betray the will of your own people

Come together
People of Africa,
Stand in a single file
Facing the same direction
In one voice sing: "God bless Africa".
For this is Africa you yearned so long living
But forget not in your song
All those who wished to sing with you

Whose souls and bodies were separated by the ruthless bullets
before sunrise
Sing with them: 'God bless Africa'.

All started with marriage

It all started with marriage:
X married P, a child was born
A Mozambican married a Portuguese, a child was born
A Briton married a Zimbabwean, a child was born
A Tswana married a Malawian, a child was born
A Turkish married a Nigerian, a child was born
A Chinese married a Cameroonian, a child was born
A Kenyan married an American, a child was born
A Namibian married an Australian, a child was born
A European married an African, a child was born
An African married an Asian, a child was born
An Australian married an American, a child was born

Through marriage of nations, oneness was born
Through marriage of different continents, oneness was born
Through marriage of different colors, oneness was born

Through marriage of cultures, the boundedness of culture
was ruined
Through marriage of ideas, tolerance was born
Through marriage of different sexes, growth was born
Let this be real growth
A growth towards peace and love

Afghanistan Vista

Hear the news!
Broadcasted from the corridors and walls of the Afghan

The war is on the bomb rattle
The people thrown into the air like torn papers in a whirlwind
The ears of the young deafened by the grenade blasts
The noses of the aged chocked in the smoke of bomb
detonations

Peace talks, peace talks, illusory peace talks!
That sends rebels cling to a foam dream
Whose pebbles dismantle in a wind's blow
Only to shatter the rebels' dreams
And vent their anger to zenith

Hear the next morning!
'All roads to the capital barricaded
The white house all ashes
Banks looted
Schools closed', denying children the right to feed their
intellects

Elegance, Obama's US interventions
Efforts
To lit a fire of real peace talks?
And the whole world listens, thoughtfully
As the talks go on
This is the end of the bulletin,

Stay tune!

A cry for freedom

How all desire to quench
The desire of the heart
To snatch light from darkness
To pluck joy from terror
To raise hope from deep seams of hopelessness

How at the dawn of the new era to begin
To nurse my dying away hope
To navigate through thread-stitched emotions
To fly on the wings of love
To command speech to take over silence
To terrorize with peace the dungeons and crevices of
weapons of mass destruction
And fight all tears with laughter

How the past to drift
To arrest oppression in handcuffs
To reclaim our freedom stolen away by hard-nosed dictators
To confront all injustice without fear
To drive away all snag into the dustbin of oblivion
To embrace freedom with adoration
To resurrect justice and equality
And with the so-called planned hope
To capture all tribulations in a cry for freedom?
Mine is a cry for freedom

On the death bed

Groaning
In his mud falling hut
On a tattered reed mat
His body only bones
His belly a wasp waist
His cheeks dreary and weary
His legs needle-like mosquito limbs
His face only a smoke screen
Visible only the rugged terrain with boulders and contours of
shrunken flesh

As I drew nearer
Gripping agony in his voice
He murmurs
To us all his children and grandchildren:
'Hear my voice well, you callous children!
In this cave-like hut I stay, as if my children are poor
With pigs I eat, as if my children are poor
Shirk rugs I wear, as if my children are poor
Bare footed I walk, as if my children are poor
Lonely I live, as if I did not bear children'

Now quote my words, the words of a dying horse:
'I don't want, and I don't want
A treasured casket for body
Glittering flowers for my grave
Cement plastered on the walls of my house
I don't want

For I can't bear to steep in a cemented grace,
I can't
For years you deserted my body
For years you did not clothe my body
For years you did not feed my body
For years you did not shelter my body
No,
I don't want a special grave!'

Children of Africa

Take heed!
Children of Africa
For words of advice value more than a piece of gold

Hear now children of Africa:
It's well known
That a soldier depends on weapon for victory in war
That a mango tree only bears mango fruits
That a young one of a snake is also a snake
That a woman can only be a widow after her husband's death
And a woman be a mother after giving birth to a child

Yet while we might be aware of these truisms
You might still be blinded
To see what is beyond their shadows
And know one most important thing
That education is as important as were cattle to the Masai
ancestors
That education is as important as were shifting cultivation to
the Bemba ancestors
That education is as important as were hunting to the San
ancestors

Take heed!
You children of Africa
Let it be printed at the core of your hearts
That education liberates
That education defends

That education enlivens
That education enriches
That education frees the mind-kidnapped by the hunches of
ignorance

Take heed children of Africa
Take heed
For if not you will be caught bathing once again by the West!

The way it is

I will only come to know the way it is
When I get there
Some say:
There is eternal peace, joy and all good life
But only for the morally upright
Others say:
Enjoy your life as much as you can
While still in this bodily camouflage
For beyond this life there is no other life

Yet more others say: It's all hell
Moaning and eternal fire that does not extinguish

Who, then, is true?
Who shall I listen to?
After all none of them has ever gone and come
I will come to know the way it is when I get there
For a man cannot cross a river before he gets there
I will come to know the way it is when I get there

Treacherous species

Everywhere they speak the same language
Rhetoric
Propaganda
The core of their manifestos
Treacherous species

They preach what they don't practice
They promise what they don't deliver
They give what is not theirs
They teach what they really don't know
Treacherous species!

When shall they learn:
To practice what they preach
To fulfill what they promise
To give what is theirs
To teach what they know
Treacherous species!
Peace! Peace! They preach
When they do the opposite
Love! Love! They encourage others
When they do the opposite
They say in God we trust
When in devil they trust
And with devil they dine
Hypocrites
Treacherous species!

Street Kid

It has been a long fruitless day
Toiling from one side of the street to the other
But getting hardly enough
To quench the thirst that burns my throat
And satiate the hunger that haunts me all life

Street kid is my name
No sister
No brother
No mother
Worse a father
My house all street

The sun my only friend now vacates
Leaving me in the open
Me the son of the street, Street kid
Prepared not to meet its sister, Cold night
That asks birth certificates even to me son of the street
And I tell her: 'I am Street kid pardon me'
Yet unforgiving she is

Born there in the street
My mother unknown diamond-hearted woman
My father unknown I don't care
I have nothing to claim
Except this hopeless life

And bruised body
Full of all kinds of wounds- fresh, dry, soaring and healing
All on one body

Seated there watching
A mother and a father with their child in between
I wish I were born of a woman
Loving and caring
And of a father
Responsible and feeling
For mine is not life
That any man deserves
Or wish to live any single moment
Only if wishes were horses!

Troubles of my heart

I

My heart bleeds
My head aches
My stomach rumbles
When I remember what they did to my forefathers

They labeled them black when in fact they are chocolate
They labeled themselves white when in fact they are pink
All to associate themselves with purity

They pushed them to the barren sand soils
And they called this development
They tipped on themselves the land full of minerals
And they called this exploration

They forced them to despise their own culture
And they called this civilization
What development?
What exploration?
What civilization?
My heart bleeds

They called them a dark continent
When in fact they were the cradle of mankind
They called them the silent majority
When they in fact were the murmuring discontented majority
They called them tea boys
When in fact they were fathers to their own children

They called them house girls
When in fact they were mothers to their own children
They called them terrorists
When in fact they were fighting for the will of the majority
Sons and daughters of the soil
Resisting oppression of the majority by the minority
Fighting for everyone's peace them included
Fighting for the land of their forefathers, sons and daughters of the soil
To clear away sins of the imperialists they pitted against the innocent of this land
No wonder:
My heart bleeds
When I remember what they did to my forefathers

II

Now that minority rule has gone
Reconciliation has been preached
Democracy has replaced autocracy
Peace has replaced war
Unity has replaced segregation
Love has been preached
Let this world be one
With a common goal
Of promoting unity between races
Of promoting lasting peace
Of denouncing oppression of man by another man
Of upholding unconditional love

It is only after this
That a bleeding heart heals
That a caricatured persona forgets
That discontented majority are contented
That those who fight for true peace down their tools
Otherwise my heart will always bleed

At the mine

(For mine workers in South Africa)

In this place!
Where there is no sentimentality for the worker
Where minerals value more than life
Where a worker kills a fellow worker
Where a master kills a fellow servant

Extremists!
Eat,
They eat until they eat no more
Drink,
They drink until they drink no more

In this place!
Where immorality breeds vice
Where men forget their families
Where women exchange their bodies for a glass of beer
Where money value more than life

Fortune seekers,
They get it!
But before dawn
The irate fortune seekers
Plug bullet in their bellies
Directing their souls to that other world
That everyone contemplates

By the Indian Ocean

As the day came
There we stood
My friend and I
Singing of the ocean that roars and mounts
Sending its massive waters home and away

A few inches away
The crouching lion-like waters halt
Squeezing into the wall where the ocean ends and starts
To captivate our attention
That we fall in as prey

There,
We sing of the waters that produce all sounds:
Like lions they roar
Like sheep they bleat
Like cocks they crow
Like bones they rattle and prattle

Staring, I say to my friend:
'There is more than the water and sand that run-stitch deep
The fish
The crabs
The snakes
And you name it
All in one house'

There, we sing
Of the waters that neither satiate their hunger nor quench their thirsty
Of the waters that hold tight all that tempers around
And I say to my friend:
'This is where they threw my grandfather'
He replies not but nods his head

There we stood
Singing of the waters that preserve meat
Singing of the waters that give taste to food
And I say to my friend: 'These are the waters that produce salt'
He replies not but nods his head

There we stood
Singing of the waters that carry large vessels
Ships, boats and canoes- all ride at pleasure
And I say to my friend: 'These are the waters that bring bulk products'
He replies not but nods his head
Stunned and baffled
By the strange waters

Babies of this world

Whether black, red, white, yellow or colored
Whether Portuguese, English, Chinese, Swahili or French
Whether male, female or hermaphrodite
They speak the same language- cry
When hungry, their language is cry
When thirsty, their language is cry

When tired, their language is cry
When angry, their language is cry
When in need of a bath, their language is cry

Tender as they are
They speak the same language- cry
The language of babies of this world!

November 2008

(For xenophobia attacks in South Africa)

I peeped through the hole
As I saw them passing through the nearby road
Men and women of all ages
Knobkerries on their shoulders
Riffles in their waists
Knives in their pockets
Malady of hatred printed all over their faces
I heard them as they passed:
'They come all the way from their motherland to take away
our jobs.
We can't tolerate this!'

I only knew I was still alive
After they had passed on
And I whispered to myself: 'Merciless fellow humans
Who fight a brother for a slice of bread
And other nations for a land they did not create
Fellow humans who forget so easily
That barely two decades ago they were scattered sheep all
over Africa
Some in the refugee camps
Others pleading with Africa to form allies'

'Through the sweat of their fallen heroes
Through the sweat of heroes from all over Africa
Through the sweat of heroes from all over the world
They all enjoy

Making marry from dawn to dusk
Smoking *ganja* until they forget their names
Drinking until they forget where they got their freedom'

There I stood nerved-'dead'
Unmoved, only following with my eyes
As I saw them entering the yard of my neighbor
'*Mukwerekwere*- foreigner, come out!'- They shouted

No questioning time
Sparks of brutal knobkerries
With my ears I heard: 'Take everything, then fire!'
No courage to keep watching
For my fellow neighbor was now history
His little house only ashes

Alas!
All the way to South Africa
To witnesses these demolitions
This death
This horror
The atrocities of xenophobia!

June 2008

(For the fallen friends and relatives during the 2008 elections in Zimbabwe)

These are the fallen heroes of the new millennium
Sons and daughters of the soil who fell fighting for true democracy
To express the views of their hearts
And to open the skulls of their heads

Ruthlessness of the juice of politics!
Bad politics!
That teaches bad thinking
That he who differs in opinion is an enemy
That he who supports another party is an enemy
Though a brother
Though a sister
Though a father
Though a mother
Shameless beings
Perpetrators of violence
Who distil flame with petroleum
To fossilize the bones of their fellow comrades

Shameless beings
Who remind our fathers of the horror of AK
Who set ablaze the houses of their neighbors in the broad day light
Who butcher the flesh of the bodies of their fellow countrymen

Who beat elders in the presence of minors
Only to teach them bad character

Some calling: '*Ngozi* beware!'
They never heard
For their ears were filled in with concrete stones
And their souls thirst for human blood

Specialists of rhetoric
Good for nothing other than speech and utterances of doom
Lying to their followers
That Messiah will never come
Worse still:
Messengers of hope and real peace
Messengers of freedom and real will of the people

I mourn my brother Mberikunashe
Who died a painful death
Threshed
Spat on
Salted on his wounds
Pinned '*mbiradzakondo*'
To ashes they burnt
Even his bones
I mourn my brother
Ashes!

What they say I am

You are a river
Winding all the way to the sea
Never mistaken to lose direction
Winding
Cutting through the edges of all rocks
Following systematically the arches of gradient

You are a chameleon
Slow but sure of every pace
Slow in movement but fast in clothing
To assume camouflage that shows power over environment
Camouflage that barricades your territory from all enemies
Imprisoning all reeds and sand

You are a tortoise
Old but never show
Soft in moving but hard to crack
Small in size but think wise

You are a fish eagle
That sees from above
Whose sight penetrates deep into great waters
To fish out reluctant fish from the deep waters

You are a cat
That sees well in the night
Whose venom more concentrated than the cobra's
Whose thinking sharper than rat smell

You are a star
Shinning in the dark night
Fighting the night darkness
To bring light on the earth
Shining you go

Before sunrise

(For Sarah and Enock, my parents)

You departed so early before sunrise
Leaving us behind with milk on the nose
Too young to think for ourselves
But certainly not by your desire, not by your wish
For it was planned by the councilors of heaven
That you shall leave before sunrise

Young though from you we learned:
Untiring love that no peevish wind shall blow away
Hard work that shall always be rewarded
True determination and courage that shall always succeed
Your legacy, the pillars of good life

May I remind you:
That the love you planted in us is a palace built on a rock
That the spirit of hard work you planted in us, no sullen
desert sun shall wither
That the true determination and courage you taught, no
mugger shall steal away
That the flowers of good life you set, not even the singe
desert weather shall shrivel
Nor summer sultry sun shall wilt

I owe you more than these words but please accept them
For it was neither my wish nor your desire
That you depart so early before sunrise
After all it is always my fervent hope

To meet you once again and forever
Breaking into a dance, joyous dance
For I know you are in a good place where you are

Mother, father, I owe you more than these words
But accept them, I plead
For your embracing yields in me eternal comfort
And your acceptance yields in me eternal hope

This is a dedication to you father and mother
A dedication from all your children
To remember you now and forever
For you shall always remain role models to us all
Though you departed before sunrise

When love dies

At the beginning we were infatuated
With great hope and exhilaration
To fuse the marvel of love and life
My capacity to give and loved heightened to the horizon

Precious moments:
Sharing our intimacies
Sharing each other's personal worldviews
Sharing our charms and joys
Experiencing the pleasures of loving and being loved
Creating a shared world of common understanding and
mutual referencing

Settling down our relationship
Reinforcing nourishing the intimacies and relations
Of every day that passes

Death of love:
A new twist, a new turn!
One among the most difficult emotional experience to bear
Nerve-numbing experience
As I try to negotiate the intense feelings of disappointment,
lost and failure

Through misunderstanding
Through betrayal
Through infidelity
Through mistrust

Through mischief
Through lack of real commitment?

Another twist:
Conflicting desire to act in the children's best interests
To re-romanticize our love
To recall the early stages of our love
To forget the pain and agony
That nurtured the death of our love
To heal the wounds that our break-up fostered
To reignite our passion for each other
When loves dies

To my husband, Farai

I

Everywhere I am bound
Bound in chains, heavy chains!
Chains of oppression
All in the name of culture

Is it a curse on this land to be born a woman?
Is it the will of God for a woman to serve men?
Is it by God's desire for a woman to kneel down before man?
Or it's by men's desire?
I was born a 'girl'
A girl to my father and mother
To me they taught:
'Your world is home
Kitchen is your industry'

I grew up knowing not that which is beyond the mountains
For my world was nothing more than home

My brother, Musa
A toddler they liberated into the big world
A world bigger than my world home!
To him they taught:
'Think beyond home
Go! Go!
For the sky is the limit'

Deep down my heart
A little questioning voice:
'But what makes you a servant of home
....and Musa a liberated explorer?'
For my forefathers' sake and for respect of their culture
The voice I resisted
For they would say:
'This child is an outcast!
This child is a curse to the ancestors!'

II

Here I am
Seated besides the bed in our little hut
Thinking badly about you

After receiving this letter of you with the words:
'Chipo, I love you my sweetheart
But I want to find everything at home in good order
Or else you risk...'

I read the letter a hundred times
Word by word, line by line
Quietly
As I hear my little daughter, Rudo snoring
In peace not knowing the oppression of culture that her future holds

And......
I begin to think, and think

My daughter and only daughter, Rudo
Should I raise you the way my mother raised me
To teach you the philosophy of submission
To teach you that home is your world
And kitchen your industry?

Again,
I read the letter
This time loudly as if reading to an audience
'…I want to find everything in good order
….Or you risk…'
I couldn't finish the lines
Fighting back my thick bloody tears dropping on the lines
To erase the agony the lines paste against me

But it's not over
The words of my husband are registered
Deep at the bottom of my heart
And my childhood memories keep on lingering
Imprinted in the sub-conscience of my consciousness
The profound depths of my mind

My husband!
Farai is his name, Rejoice
Who to rejoice if not only men
In this terrible world where culture favors only men?

III

Yes,

I am happy my husband, Farai has come!
After months in the city
Toiling for me his family
A lovely caring husband
More caring than my mother to me
When I was still little Chipo, the toddler
A man who sacrifice his life for family
Here he comes, Farai!

Farai, my darling!
What are in all these big bags?
Too heavy for a woman to carry
Peeping I unequivocally asks:
'Did you bring the whole city for me?
Groceries, clothes and a big radio
For little Rudo and I to listen
When you are away, far away from home
Too big things for a woman's hands!'
 At the back of my mind
That little voice persists
Mocking as if directing to a fool:
'You foolish woman! Poor you!
 If you go to the city you can bring all this
And you forget toiling all day in your industry, kitchen
Go! You will leave this poor world'

I try, try to resist the voice
Too powerful a voice!

Enough to leave me open-mouthed
For Farai to notice
And to ask: 'What's the matter my love?'
'Don't I also have the right to go and work for myself in the city
To cease being a servant for your home?'

Bewildered, dumfounded
With bloodshot Cyclopean stare
Myself akimbo
Ready for anything-the unknown

The reply to my wife, Chipo

I

Chipo, my wife!
Listen and listen carefully

When I was a child you were also a child
You grew in the same village as I
Where you were taught that it's not a curse to be born a
woman
And neither is it a fortune to be born a man
For both have their own merits as demerits

Chipo, my wife
You were taught I am sure you were taught
That the words 'man' and 'woman' are cultural constructions
Pinned down to distinguish the human of your nature from
mine

Chipo, my wife
I am sure you know, this you know
That man is born physically stronger than a woman
Though perhaps not all men
To bear the harshness of the world beyond home
And to resist the forces against the will of his power

Chipo, my wife
You were taught I am sure you were taught
That a woman's world is home
And a man's world is beyond home

For our forefathers and ancestors were not fools
Neither were they half-backed thinkers
But knew for certain
That man's power though limited has an inner determination
Determination to explore other worlds beyond home

Chipo, listen!
It's not by my design
Neither was it by our ancestors' desire
To see women oppressed by men
Or men by women
For the ancestors are not only men
But revered men and women of value and character
Who always embraced peace and love
And in love and peace they all lived
Men and women

II
Now,
I can peep through glazing into your deep-seated heart
Dissecting it into two huge pieces
And I see………
You are a lovely woman of my heart
Troubled to the core of your heart
And to the back of your mind
Yes, I see!
That you are a woman
Eaten away by the tradition and culture of our forefathers

Surprised ever I am
That you fight the truth you know
That all we claim ownership to is heritage
Heritage that we inherited from our forefathers
Heritage we shall pass on to posterity
Heritage we shall pass on to our children's children
That they grow up singing:
'Papa and mama divided us roles to play
Scared roles that should not be confused
Lest we confuse our minds
And become a senseless people
A people with no culture
A people with no tradition
A people with nowhere to fall back at

Ours is a tradition that was created out of ages
A tradition built on rocky wisdom
A tradition nurtured by accumulated experiences

Rejoice, therefore, rejoice
For what you are
For what we are!

III

Listen now listen!
Carefully:
It's not all that easy out there
There beyond the world home
For in terrible weather I suffer

For in industry I toil all day
Suffering and toiling for you, family

Confuse the roles
Go, work in the industry
As I look after the world home
And see if you will regret not
And learn an unforgettable lesson
That a flickering tongue always burdens the bearer

Let this be printed in your heart
That the designer-Creator knew
When for partners he created
A weaker sex and a stronger sex
The two to live together
For life
For one is endowed with a heart of love
And the other a heart of endurance

Follow therefore the command of the Creator
The will of nature
Follow!
Lest you are tempted to think wrong
That a fig tree can bear oranges
That a man can conceive and carry pregnancy
That you are wiser than he who created you

Corruption

All the house is dirty
Inside and outside flies are buzzing
With dry throats and searching noses
To suck the juice of all dirty

Yet,
Tantalizing is their hopes
Unquenched is their thirst
Unsatiated is their hunger
All perched high on the zenith
Go to the road, you meet them
Lining up cars like ants in approaching summer

Go to the banks, you meet them
Forging signatures and piling money like papers

Go to learning institutions, you meet them
Practicing rent seeking of all kinds

Go to the courts of law, you meet them
Paying kickbacks buying favors of prosecutors and judges

Go to passport offices, you meet them
Seeking bribes from their clients, poor clients

Uuuum!
All the house is dirty
Inside and outside flies are buzzing

With dry throats and searching noses
To suck the juice of all dirty, rubbish!

New media technology

I am new media technology
An inexorably complex entity
A spider web that has spread its tentacles
Reaching all corners of the world
Making the world a BIG one world

I am new media technology
Whose impact everyone has been felt
Positively or otherwise

For those proud of and make use of me for the good
Jobs they get through me
Messages they send through me
Games they watch through me
In banks transactions they make through me
New media technology

I am new media technology
Vulnerable I am
Manipulated many times to put others at risk
For some jobs they lose in my name
For others money they lose in my name
And for yet others relations they serve in my name
New media technology

I am new media technology
A new culture
Invented to dislodge the old

To make some happy all life
And others cheerless all life

My life as a woman

I am a controversial figure among many
A talk of everyone in the "modern" world
A woman in patriarch!

But let me say it out by myself:
A woman in patriarch is like a child born into a culture
Or into a world blessed or cursed

I might be born a poor girl, poor to the bone
With barely nothing to call "my property"
My life miserable like that of a beggar
Only to turn out a millionaire
And to change my status from poor girl to rich madam
The very moment I get married to a millionaire

I am always perplexed when I hear those who say:
A woman in patriarch is always cursed
For she is born to inherit
And though sometimes to inherit poverty
But only imagine where she inherits treasury!
Isn't this blessed a life?

Death of the rural home

Countryside is lamenting
Mourning his beloved children
Who like cockroaches to milk have gone for good
And like arrows in the mist have disappeared for good
They are nowhere in sight!

Countryside is lamenting
Mourning his children's dilapidating homesteads
Falling in desolation
With no one to reconstruct their walls
Or to take care of their plummeting fences
African city, the betrayer of the countryside

African city, the merciless annihilator
In silence you incite and celebrate death of the rural home!
Impoverishing countryside your brother
Depriving him of his resources, manpower
To enrich your palaces there, far
But only in numbers
For in resources you dwindle
In fear of their numbers
As like iron filings they come without ceasing

Countryside is crying
Expressing his displeasure before his sister, Urban
Who is never ashamed
Of robbing sons and daughters of her own brother
Urban, a witch to your brother you are

For like capitalism that bewitches the poor in day light
And colonialist that terrorize in the name of civilization
You are never ashamed of your dirt works

Death of the rural home
Lonely and deserted
Is all what Urban cherishes!

Worlds of this world

There are many worlds in this world
Too many to count!
Many times we pass through them but unknowingly
Many times we see them but blindfolded to see
Many times we touch them but paralyzed to feel
Many times we smell them but our noses so overwhelmed to
pick up their scent
Many times we think of them but too strong they are to slip
away the banalities of imagination
Yet the truth remains
That there are many worlds in this world
Guess which worlds!

Harurwa

The drinker of rainwater
The sucker of morning dew
Harurwa
You are the earner of local and foreign currency
Friend to vegetation- all that is green
Though the green you don't feed on but live with
Lover of culture and tradition
Source of inspiration to lovers of research
For yourself you 've earned
The best of all names "golden fly"
For you are not only gold for those humans who depend on you
But both to vegetation and the people
Though to predators an enemy you are
And to those who see you not as an equal being unfriendly you are

Golden fly, edible green bugs, I call you
Not edible stinkbugs as they used to call you
As if you to everyone, even your friends

I and not I alone
Salute you home and away
The irresistible delicacy of many
The conservation player of all ages
The preserver of all cultural norms
All praises
You deserve!

African City

I am afraid, anxious, happy and sad
All these contradictions in me they live
For I live in a place where anything goes
The African City
Though others say: "The Western City too!"

In you anything goes
Good, bad, desirable, undesirable, humane and inhumane
Like fire you burn everything that enters your territory
Like an ocean you are gullible to everything that enters your
mouth
All races in you they dance
All car models in you they run
All gases in you they blow
All languages in you they speak
All currencies in you they circulate
All cultures in you they mingle
A melting pot where anything goes!

Your biggest promoters!
Capitalists
Everywhere they speak well about you:
A fountain of development
A centre of Cultural Revolution
A place where everyone mind his own business
A place where tolerance is the order of the day
A place where democracy and liberty are words so BIG
Though to confuse many

A place where all live with all

Your biggest critics!
Moralists and traditionalists- lovers of morality and tradition
Everywhere they speak badly about you:
A place where witches find refuge
A place where cultures disintegrate
A place where prostitution is a normal business
A place where robbery is a form of employment
A place where anything goes
Holly and evil

In you I am afraid
I live with all anxiety and fear of the unknown
But sometimes happy, full of hope of all good to befall me
Yet I remain always inquisitive
Slow and vigilant like a chameleon when treading
For in you anything goes!

Up there

Up there seated
Observing closely their devious, cunning steps
I saw their ferociousness descending
Fiercely like the arrow of a scorpion
Deadly like the spear of a buffalo-hornet
Corrosive like juice of the gourd
Their mouths wide open
Salivating in greediness
To devour Africa from all sides
To divide Africa asunder
Tearing her into pieces
Setting her sons and daughters into a spiral of anarchy

Like hunger they know no bounds
Their slogan:
'Throw that away and take this!
Leave your ways and follow us!
Curse your brother for he is a fool!'
All in the illusion of the rhetoric of purity

When shall the baby Africa stand and walk for herself?
Or the boy Africa grows into manhood?
And the girl Africa grows into womanhood?
That the African masses get out of the labyrinths set before
them?

Shall we go by the adage: 'history is cyclic?'
For what happened yesterday is happening today
For what Africa suffered yesterday she suffers today

For what Africa lost yesterday she loses today?

When shall you stand up Africa
And sing the song of true renaissance
That all your sons and daughters are truly renewed
Reinvigorated
Filled with new oomph to safeguard your borders from the
ominously predatory forces of imperialists
Descending once again in disguise
Now to devour the heart of Africa
And to spare no more sons and daughters of the land?

I lamented for my beloved Africa
As I saw them approaching
All in painted faces
With sweet words in their mouths
And deadly weaponry all around their bodies

Where are you the think tanks of Africa?
Where are you the technocrats of Africa?
Where are you the torch bearers of Africa?
Where are you the chancellors of Africa?
To save your sons and daughters
Before their protective shell is broken
And their lives vanquished and exterminated from the
corridors of their motherland!

Untied tongues

When summer comes to southern Africa
The sun takes charge
And when winter comes
Cold overtakes

When sun rises
All children rejoice
Coming out of their little beds
To catch sweet rays of the sun

When independence comes
All sons and daughters in bondage celebrate
And war prisoners' chains drop to their knees
Respecting the essence of the new era

Imagine what happens:
When the eyes of the blind are opened!
When the ears of the deaf are unlocked!
And the tongues of the dumb are untied!
Nothing to celebrate

All that flies fly to land?

(*A response to the poem: 'That flies lands'*)

Yes!
Little do we know
To whom these words are directed:

Ferocious darkness fills all land
Night falls all time to give no chance to day
Vicious night forgetting that it comes to go
To relieve the wracked souls of their agony
And the tired bodies of their weariness

Silent voices restless and mourning
Cry in agony, ear-splitting
Filling all the sky and heavens beyond
Hiding from us
The nostalgia and melancholy of those gone

We long to sing joy
In the sunrise
Yet like morning dew that evaporates on sunrise
And winter clouds that disappear on midday
And meat smoke that scatters so instantaneously
And bonfire smoke that staggers skywards like a drunkard
And chameleon camouflage, mobile and constantly on the
move
Everything seems to go the same way
For nothing comes to stay
Nor flies high not to land

We seem to agree!

Hitherto!
Only few and indeed a few
Question the nature of things
When they hear not only to hear
And see not only to see
That everything is in the process
Of coming to go and going to come
The process of becoming and begoing
Coming from where and going where?
Nobody knows for we all stagger in the darkness
And stumble in circle in the pelt rain
With our steps faltering, anesthetizing in the mist zone
Pulsating in the reverberation of demise
Making us at least sure that we are all definitions waiting to be
defined
By who, for who, and for what?
That's another question, a problem
Big!
That like cold bath we need to get out of it fast as we got in

We prophesy to know
That all that flies lands
But is this always the case?
That which goes around comes around?
That sun sets to rise on the morrow?
That all that flies, fly to land?
… and that all that lives, live to die?

This is food for thought to us all
And all the generations to come!

Language injustice

All of us speak
Even the speech impaired - the dumb - speak
Only that we speak different languages

From south to north
From east to west
We all speak
Different tongues and clicking sounds
But a hardly acknowledged reality, especially by our friends
from the north!
To us all their language they impose
Their definitions of color they enforce
They say they are white when in fact they are pink
They define others as black when the others are in fact
chocolate coated
Is this by design or ignorance?
That they fail to define the color of things
Even the color of their own skin!
Such, is language injustice

In schools, the story remains
They force us to change our traditional names
And to learn in their foreign languages
And encourage us to despise our own languages
That we laugh at our own people when they wrongly speak
the foreign language
That we prize our own people when they fail to speak the
language of their motherland

That we give accolades to our people when they deride their culture
That we give credit to our people when they mimic foreign cultures
And approve of our people when they speak languages unfamiliar to their own people
Such is language injustice

Rhetoric of democracy they preach
But only to reveal their hypocrisy
For where is democracy
Where is equality
When some languages are more equal than others?
Such is language injustice

Death

Death never satiates
It reaps where it never scattered a seed
And takes away even those who are unwilling to go
Death never satiates

It swallows up the old, the young, and the unborn
It snatches away the beauty and the ugly
It respects no king, no prince, no princess
It spares no creature as if it is the owner of all life
Death never satiates

If it grows fat, then death must be the fattest
If it grows strong, then death must be the strongest
If it is a warrior, then death must be the most skillful warrior
If it is a hero, then death must be the hero of all heroes
If it is a container, then death must be the biggest of all
containers

Come life, goes life
Like wind that passes by silence life is swept away
Like morning dew that evaporates at sunrise life disappears
Like bright flower that withers at midday life perishes
All in the name of death
Death never satiates!

This death that never satiates!
A fearful creature it must be
For no man, no woman can stop it

No injection, no medicine can conquer it
This death that never satiates!

A prophecy of revolution

This song travels long
Its echoes reach all corners
Flowing through even the tides of the sea
A distinct murmur to all bound in chains

Hark, hear the call!
The call of a revolutionary spirit crying for everlasting peace
Its voice earsplitting deafening even the ears of the oppressor
Shaking all ground like whirlwind blowing away all the sand
Filling the eyes of the oppressor
Loosening all the chains of the oppressed
And the yokes on their necks
And the stone walls around them

It is this moment
That the tyrant shall be conquered
That the prison guards shall be turned into prisoners as the
prisoners are liberated
That the masters shall be turned into slaves as the slaves are
liberated
That the oppressors shall bind themselves in chains and beg
the slaves to free them
All this in the split of a second and the blink of an eye
As the echoes of the revolutionary call passes by

When this time comes to pass
The oppressor shall learn a long life lesson
That all life deserves respect

That all life deserves dignity
That all life deserves freedom
That all life deserves love
That all life is revere
For it all belongs to the Creator

Children of chaos

They have heard a voice calling
A voice of chaos
Melodious and sweet but cunning
Foolishly they hearken
To join the initiations and rites of passage of chaos
Sons and daughters of chaos!

Children of chaos
All what they know is:
To resist the order of order
To invoke sorrow where there is happiness
To trigger death where there is life
To wage war where there is peace
To despise the goodness of humane morality where there is
culture
To turn men into women in protest against order of their
biology
To turn women into men in protest against order of their
creation
Lost
To pretend to call for equal rights when they are calling for
destruction of others' cultures
Sons and daughters of chaos!

Children of chaos
Loud they are
For all they long is to be heard by all world
Salivating for new converts

In disguise they come
Wearing white but black masks
You better remain vigilant you children of order
For unaware you will be caught like children bathing at the river

Children of chaos
They assume all colors like the chameleon of the forest
They use all tricks like python attracting prey
They use all weapons like soldiers in war
They shift their goal posts to win at all costs like children in game
They do the unthinkable all their life long
Sons and daughters of chaos!

Fools

They enjoy when they do foolish things
They cry when all is well
They laugh when things are bad
Fools!

Where they pass by everyone point fingers at them
For their presence is a disgrace that everyone notices
Where they eat it is all dirty
Where they sleep it is all noise
For their spirits give them no rest
Fools!

They act but don't think
They see but don't examine
They talk but don't select words
They associate but don't respect
Fools!

They love to do opposite things
Where they should be silent they make noise
Where they should make love they do with those of the same
sex
Where they should eat they eat with dirty hands
Where they should lead they take all astray
Where they should construct they destruct
Fools!

Their heads are full of water
Their morals a rubbish pit

Their existence a disgrace to society
Fools!

Songs from the forests

From all directions I hear voices
Crying voices!
Of the scattered sheep of the Promised Land
Scattered as if they have no place to call home
Surviving on petty trading as if they have no fields to farm
Sleeping in shacks as if they have no houses back home
All because of the misery that politicians evoke

From the north, from the south
From the east, from the west
The voices cry loud, strong and determined
Their echoes reaching high up the sky and into the heavens
To pray for deliverance from the owner of heaven and earth

I can see all sufferings and deaths of the scattered sheep
Instigated by a few other sheep
The few wild sheep whose minds think nothing beyond
material benefit
The few wild sheep whose hearts care nothing more than
their material wealth
The few wild sheep whose dead morals respect no lives other
than theirs

Shall these few wild sheep stand the truth
When time for their judgment comes?
They eat as if there is nothing to spare
And make merry as if the entire house is in order
Only time shall tell when their reign lasts

But certainly their evil ways will catch up with them
For the prayers of the scattered sheep are stronger than their
convictions

Africa voice

In the name of western civilization
Old age comes early for Africa

Starting with slave trade
Where daughters and sons of the land labored for nothing
Toiling day and night for nothing
Breaking the hardest rocks with their hands
Lifting the biggest rocks with their hands
Building the tallest buildings with their hands
Bound in the strongest chains all their bodies
Old age comes early for Africa

Off it went slave trade
The worst evil of Africa!
Only to be replaced with another evil
Colonialism!
Bringing back the injustices of inequality
And the ruthlessness of the tenets of slavery:
Apartheid and racism
With the colonialists labeling Africa a dark continent
With a people who had seen no light
Only to justify their imperialism
All in the name of civilization

Off it went colonialism
The worst evil of Africa!
Only to be replaced with another evil
Cultural imperialism but in the name of globalization!

Bringing back the injustices of inequality
Where some cultures are more equal than others
Labeling other cultures inferiors
Only to justify their imperialism
All in the name of civilization

Today, look what they do!
They preach democracy which they themselves never practice
They preach peace when they invoke wars and manufacture firearms
They label others undemocratic when they themselves are
They label others uncivilized when they define civilization for all others
Isn't this hypocrisy and treachery?
Is their civilization the only civilization?
And how relevant is their civilization to Africa?

2013 Catastrophe

The land is full
Pregnant with mad water

There is war
Between the sea and the land
With the sea threatening to invade land
To conquer the sons and daughters of land
To take into captivity all their possessions
Big and small
And install mermaids and crocodiles as kings and headmen

Land is invaded
Everywhere, catchments of tears and sorrow
Sea refuses to listen
Rivers refuse to take heed
They all race in rant and rave to terrorize land their enemy
To punish Land's sons and daughters for using their waters
without permission

A short while later
Land is in chains
Its sons and daughters all running amok
To the east and to the west, to the north and to the south
Trying to escape the whip of their enemy
Some escape
Others are held in chains together with their motherland
More others trapped by the border before escape
A few days later, I listen to the radio

Broadcasting:
More than seventy lives perished!
More than five billion meticals lost!
More than five billion metical needed for the victims!
A loaded burden to motherland!

Where are you policemen?

You waste time on the parade
You waste time in the beer halls
You waste time harvesting money from the roads
When the poor are all in peril
Waiting for you to arrest their number one enemy
Poverty!

Where are you policemen?
You waste time arresting people on petty crimes
Arresting those who didn't pay for their radio licenses
Arresting those who didn't pay for their bicycles to cycle on
the land
When number one criminals are by side executing their
killings
You are alerted to rescue the dying
Only to appear three house later
When you are sure the criminal has gone
Where are you policemen?

Where are you policemen
To arrest the hunger that gnaws
To arrest poverty that haunts
To arrest death that kills
To arrest ignorance that blinds
To arrest hopelessness that disempowers?

When shall you become real policemen?
Policemen who work for the people

Policemen who police those who deserve
Policemen who strive for real justice
Policemen who work for order and peace
Policemen who police with ethics
Over to you
Where are you policemen?